Jeremiah 29:11

Monthly

Motivation

Devotion

JOURNAL CALENDAR

Frizella Taylor

Unless otherwise indicated, all scripture references are from

New International Version (NIV)

Jeremiah 29:11 Monthly Motivation & Devotion Journal Calendar

© 2021 Frizella Taylor

Contributors: Corean Donegan, Deliliah Miller

ISBN# 978-1-953526-25-0

Published by TaylorMade Publishing

Jacksonville, FL

www.TaylorMadePublishingFL.com

(904) 323-1334

TaylorMade Publishing

Belongs to:

_____

Year:

_____

JEREMIAH 29:11
MONTHLY
MOTIVATION
&
DEVOTION

JOURNAL CALENDAR

Introduction

Every year, the Lord speaks to us to set a direction for the new year. He tends to give us a word to stand on and perhaps a scripture to support that word. We refer to this word throughout the year. We get revelation, application, and direction from it. We use that word and scripture to set our goals and aspirations for the year which gives us a focused target for our life.

This monthly motivation & devotion journal calendar is designed to assist you in staying organized, setting your goals, tracking your goals and ultimately, obtaining your goals.

At the start of the year, fill in the future plans section and gratitude's from the past or present that affected you positively. Each month, you will have an opportunity to write your inspirations, monthly goals, steps to achieve your goals, a full month calendar view, budget, shopping list, space to write your challenges, and monthly affirmations.

Lastly, you decide which year you want to use for this calendar. So, start in any month within the year. I pray that you enjoy your journey to reaching your goals.

MY WORD FOR THIS YEAR

MY GOALS FOR THIS YEAR

MY SCRIPTURE FOR THE YEAR

Gratitude's

January

Then the *Lord* replied:

" *Write* down the *Revelation*

and make it *Plain* on tablets

so that a *Herald* may run with it.

—Habakkuk 2:2—

Inspirations

Your thoughts, ideas, notes, hopes, goals, plans, potentials, etc....

Monthly Goals

SPIRITUAL

FAMILY

CAREER

HEALTH

Steps to Achieve My Goals

January

SUNDAY	MONDAY	TUESDAY	WEDNESDAY

Year: _____

THURSDAY	FRIDAY	SATURDAY	TO DO LIST

TO DO LIST

-
-
-
-
-
-
-
-
-

NOTES

My Budget

Monthly Income   Monthly Savings

Item Source	Amount	Date	Amount

Monthly Expenses

Item	Due Date	Amount
Rent/Mortgage		
Electric		
Gas		
Cell Phone		
Groceries		
Car Payment		
Auto Expenses		
Personal Care		
Entertainment		
Student Loans		
Credit Cards		
Miscellaneous		

Summary

Total Monthly Income	Total Monthly Expenses	Total Monthly Savings	Cash Balance

Shopping List

Grocery List	All other shopping needs

Notes:

This Month I Was Challenged to:

_____
_____
_____
_____
_____
_____
_____
_____
_____
_____
_____
_____
_____
_____
_____
_____
_____
_____

I Can do all this through _Him_ who gives me _Strength._

-Philippians 4:13-

Monthly Affirmation From God's Word:

What does God say is true about you?

I am... - I will... - God is...

_____
_____
_____
_____
_____
_____
_____
_____
_____
_____
_____
_____
_____
_____
_____

I say to myself, "The LORD is my Portion; therefore I will wait for him.

-Lamentations 3:24-

February

For *God* so loved the *World*

that he *Gave* his one and only *Son,* that

whoever *Believes* in *Him* shall not perish

but have *eternal Life.*

—John 3:16—

Inspirations

Your thoughts, ideas, notes, hopes, goals, plans, potentials, etc....

Monthly Goals

SPIRITUAL

FAMILY

CAREER

HEALTH

Steps to Achieve My Goals

February

SUNDAY	MONDAY	TUESDAY	WEDNESDAY

Year: _____

THURSDAY	FRIDAY	SATURDAY	TO DO LIST
			•
			•
			•
			•
			•
			•
			•
			•
			•
			NOTES

My Budget

Monthly Income   Monthly Savings

Item Source	Amount	Date	Amount

Monthly Expenses

Item	Due Date	Amount
Rent/Mortgage		
Electric		
Gas		
Cell Phone		
Groceries		
Car Payment		
Auto Expenses		
Personal Care		
Entertainment		
Student Loans		
Credit Cards		
Miscellaneous		

Summary

Total Monthly Income	Total Monthly Expenses	Total Monthly Savings	Cash Balance

Shopping List

Grocery List

All other shopping needs

Notes:

This Month I Was Challenged to:

_____

_____

_____

_____

_____

_____

_____

_____

_____

_____

_____

_____

_____

_____

_____

_____

_____

_____

I Can do all this through *Him* who gives me *Strength.*

-Philippians 4:13-

Monthly Affirmation From God's Word:

What does God say is true about you?

I am... - I will... - God is...

_____
_____
_____
_____
_____
_____
_____
_____
_____
_____
_____
_____
_____
_____
_____
_____
_____

I say to myself, "The *LORD* is my *Portion*; therefore I will wait for him.

-Lamentations 3:24-

March

Faithfulness *Springs* forth from

the *Earth,* and righteousness

looks down from *Heaven.*

—Psalm 85:11—

Inspirations

Your thoughts, ideas, notes, hopes, goals, plans, potentials, etc....

Monthly Goals

SPIRITUAL

FAMILY

CAREER

HEALTH

Steps to Achieve My Goals

March

SUNDAY	MONDAY	TUESDAY	WEDNESDAY

Year: _____

THURSDAY	FRIDAY	SATURDAY	TO DO LIST

NOTES

My Budget

Monthly Income   Monthly Savings

Item Source	Amount	Date	Amount

Monthly Expenses

Item	Due Date	Amount
Rent/Mortgage		
Electric		
Gas		
Cell Phone		
Groceries		
Car Payment		
Auto Expenses		
Personal Care		
Entertainment		
Student Loans		
Credit Cards		
Miscellaneous		

Summary

Total Monthly Income	Total Monthly Expenses	Total Monthly Savings	Cash Balance

Shopping List

Grocery List	All other shopping needs

Notes:

This Month I Was Challenged to:

_____

_____

_____

_____

_____

_____

_____

_____

_____

_____

_____

_____

_____

_____

_____

_____

_____

I Can do all this through *Him* who gives me *Strength.*

-Philippians 4:13-

Monthly Affirmation From God's Word:

What does God say is true about you?

I am... - I will... - God is...

_____

_____

_____

_____

_____

_____

_____

_____

_____

_____

_____

_____

_____

_____

_____

_____

_____

I say to myself, "The LORD is my Portion; therefore I will wait for him.

-Lamentations 3:24-

April

May *he* be like *rain*

falling on a mown field,

like *showers* watering the earth.

—Psalm 72:6—

Inspirations

Your thoughts, ideas, notes, hopes, goals, plans, potentials, etc....

Monthly Goals

SPIRITUAL

FAMILY

CAREER

HEALTH

Steps to Achieve My Goals

April

SUNDAY	MONDAY	TUESDAY	WEDNESDAY

Year: _____

THURSDAY	FRIDAY	SATURDAY	TO DO LIST

-
-
-
-
-
-
-
-
-

NOTES

My Budget

Monthly Income		Monthly Savings	

Item Source	Amount	Date	Amount

Monthly Expenses

Item	Due Date	Amount
Rent/Mortgage		
Electric		
Gas		
Cell Phone		
Groceries		
Car Payment		
Auto Expenses		
Personal Care		
Entertainment		
Student Loans		
Credit Cards		
Miscellaneous		

Summary

Total Monthly Income	Total Monthly Expenses	Total Monthly Savings	Cash Balance

Shopping List

Grocery List   All other shopping needs

Notes:

This Month I Was Challenged to:

_____

_____

_____

_____

_____

_____

_____

_____

_____

_____

_____

_____

_____

_____

_____

_____

_____

I Can do all this through *Him* who gives me *Strength.*

-Philippians 4:13-

Monthly Affirmation From God's Word:

What does God say is true about you?

I am... - I will... - God is...

_____

_____

_____

_____

_____

_____

_____

_____

_____

_____

_____

_____

_____

_____

_____

_____

_____

_____

I say to myself, "The LORD is my Portion; therefore I will wait for him.

-Lamentations 3:24-

May

In his days *may* the righteous

Flourish and *Prosperity*

abound till the moon is no more.

—Psalm 72:7—

Inspirations

Your thoughts, ideas, notes, hopes, goals, plans, potentials, etc....

Monthly Goals

SPIRITUAL

FAMILY

CAREER

HEALTH

Steps to Achieve My Goals

May

SUNDAY	MONDAY	TUESDAY	WEDNESDAY

May

THURSDAY	FRIDAY	SATURDAY	TO DO LIST
			•
			•
			•
			•
			•
			•
			•
			•
			•
			NOTES

My Budget

Monthly Income   Monthly Savings

Item Source	Amount	Date	Amount

Monthly Expenses

Item	Due Date	Amount
Rent/Mortgage		
Electric		
Gas		
Cell Phone		
Groceries		
Car Payment		
Auto Expenses		
Personal Care		
Entertainment		
Student Loans		
Credit Cards		
Miscellaneous		

Summary

Total Monthly Income	Total Monthly Expenses	Total Monthly Savings	Cash Balance

Shopping List

Grocery List

All other shopping needs

Notes:

This Month I Was Challenged to:

_____
_____
_____
_____
_____
_____
_____
_____
_____
_____
_____
_____
_____
_____
_____
_____
_____

I Can do all this through *Him* who gives me *Strength.*

-Philippians 4:13-

Monthly Affirmation From God's Word:

What does God say is true about you?

I am... - I will... - God is...

_____

_____

_____

_____

_____

_____

_____

_____

_____

_____

_____

_____

_____

_____

_____

_____

_____

_____

I say to myself, "The _LORD_ is my _Portion_; therefore I will wait for him.

-Lamentations 3:24-

June

I saw the *Holy City*, the new

Jerusalem, coming down out of

heaven from *God*, prepared as

a *Bride* beautifully dressed

for her *Husband.*

—Revelation 21:2—

Inspirations

Your thoughts, ideas, notes, hopes, goals, plans, potentials, etc....

Monthly Goals

SPIRITUAL

FAMILY

CAREER

HEALTH

Steps to Achieve My Goals

June

SUNDAY	MONDAY	TUESDAY	WEDNESDAY

Year: _____

THURSDAY	FRIDAY	SATURDAY	TO DO LIST
			•
			•
			•
			•
			•
			•
			•
			•
			•
			NOTES

Monthly Income

Monthly Savings

Item Source	Amount	Date	Amount

Monthly Expenses

Item	Due Date	Amount
Rent/Mortgage		
Electric		
Gas		
Cell Phone		
Groceries		
Car Payment		
Auto Expenses		
Personal Care		
Entertainment		
Student Loans		
Credit Cards		
Miscellaneous		

Summary

Total Monthly Income	Total Monthly Expenses	Total Monthly Savings	Cash Balance

Shopping List

Grocery List	All other shopping needs

Notes:

This Month I Was Challenged to:

_____

_____

_____

_____

_____

_____

_____

_____

_____

_____

_____

_____

_____

_____

_____

_____

_____

_____

I Can do all this through *Him* who gives me *Strength.*

-Philippians 4:13-

Monthly Affirmation From God's Word:

What does God say is true about you?

I am... - I will... - God is...

_____

_____

_____

_____

_____

_____

_____

_____

_____

_____

_____

_____

_____

_____

_____

_____

_____

_____

I say to myself, "The _LORD_ is my _Portion_; therefore I will wait for him.

-Lamentations 3:24-

July

At last we have *Freedom*, for

Christ has set us free!

We must always cherish this *Truth*

and firmly *Refuse* to go back

into the *Bondage* of our *Past*.

—Galatians 5:1—

Inspirations

Your thoughts, ideas, notes, hopes, goals, plans, potentials, etc....

Monthly Goals

SPIRITUAL

FAMILY

CAREER

HEALTH

Steps to Achieve My Goals

July

SUNDAY	MONDAY	TUESDAY	WEDNESDAY

THURSDAY	FRIDAY	SATURDAY	TO DO LIST
			•
			•
			•
			•
			•
			•
			•
			•
			•
			NOTES

My Budget

Monthly Income   **Monthly Savings**

Item Source	Amount	Date	Amount

Monthly Expenses

Item	Due Date	Amount
Rent/Mortgage		
Electric		
Gas		
Cell Phone		
Groceries		
Car Payment		
Auto Expenses		
Personal Care		
Entertainment		
Student Loans		
Credit Cards		
Miscellaneous		

Summary

Total Monthly Income	Total Monthly Expenses	Total Monthly Savings	Cash Balance

Shopping List

Grocery List	All other shopping needs

Notes:

This Month I Was Challenged to:

_____

_____

_____

_____

_____

_____

_____

_____

_____

_____

_____

_____

_____

_____

I Can do all this through *Him* who gives me *Strength.*

-Philippians 4:13-

Monthly Affirmation From God's Word:

What does God say is true about you?

I am... - I will... - God is...

_____

_____

_____

_____

_____

_____

_____

_____

_____

_____

_____

_____

_____

_____

_____

_____

_____

_____

I say to myself, "The LORD is my Portion; therefore I will wait for him.

-Lamentations 3:24-

August

Then he said to his disciples,

"The *Harvest* is plentiful but

the *Workers* are few.

Ask the Lord of the *Harvest*, therefore,

to send out *Workers* into

his *Harvest* field." .

—Matthew 9:37-38—

Inspirations

Your thoughts, ideas, notes, hopes, goals, plans, potentials, etc....

Monthly Goals

SPIRITUAL

FAMILY

CAREER

HEALTH

Steps to Achieve My Goals

August

SUNDAY	MONDAY	TUESDAY	WEDNESDAY

August

Year: _____

THURSDAY	FRIDAY	SATURDAY	TO DO LIST
			•
			•
			•
			•
			•
			•
			•
			•
			•
			NOTES

My Budget

Monthly Income   **Monthly Savings**

Item Source	Amount	Date	Amount

Monthly Expenses

Item	Due Date	Amount
Rent/Mortgage		
Electric		
Gas		
Cell Phone		
Groceries		
Car Payment		
Auto Expenses		
Personal Care		
Entertainment		
Student Loans		
Credit Cards		
Miscellaneous		

Summary

Total Monthly Income	Total Monthly Expenses	Total Monthly Savings	Cash Balance

Shopping List

Grocery List   All other shopping needs

Notes:

This Month I Was Challenged to:

_____

_____

_____

_____

_____

_____

_____

_____

_____

_____

_____

_____

_____

_____

_____

_____

_____

_____

_____

I Can do all this through *Him* who gives me *Strength.*

-Philippians 4:13-

Monthly Affirmation From God's Word:

What does God say is true about you?

I am... - I will... - God is...

_____

_____

_____

_____

_____

_____

_____

_____

_____

_____

_____

_____

_____

_____

_____

_____

_____

_____

_____

I say to myself, "The *LORD* is my *Portion*; therefore I will wait for him.

-Lamentations 3:24-

September

Behold, the *Former* things have

come to *Pass*,

And *New Things* I declare;

Before they *Spring* forth

I tell you of them."

—Isaiah 42:9—

Inspirations

Your thoughts, ideas, notes, hopes, goals, plans, potentials, etc....

Monthly Goals

SPIRITUAL

FAMILY

CAREER

HEALTH

Steps to Achieve My Goals

September

SUNDAY	MONDAY	TUESDAY	WEDNESDAY

Year: _____

THURSDAY	FRIDAY	SATURDAY	TO DO LIST
			•
			•
			•
			•
			•
			•
			•
			•
			•

NOTES

My Budget

Monthly Income   Monthly Savings

Item Source	Amount	Date	Amount

Monthly Expenses

Item	Due Date	Amount
Rent/Mortgage		
Electric		
Gas		
Cell Phone		
Groceries		
Car Payment		
Auto Expenses		
Personal Care		
Entertainment		
Student Loans		
Credit Cards		
Miscellaneous		

Summary

Total Monthly Income	Total Monthly Expenses	Total Monthly Savings	Cash Balance

Shopping List

Grocery List	All other shopping needs

Notes:

This Month I Was Challenged to:

_____

_____

_____

_____

_____

_____

_____

_____

_____

_____

_____

_____

_____

_____

_____

_____

_____

_____

I Can do all this through *Him* who gives me *Strength.*

-Philippians 4:13-

Monthly Affirmation From God's Word:

What does God say is true about you?

I am... - I will... - God is...

_____

_____

_____

_____

_____

_____

_____

_____

_____

_____

_____

_____

_____

_____

_____

_____

_____

I say to myself, "The *LORD* is my *Portion*; therefore I will wait for him.

-Lamentations 3:24-

October

This is a *Day* you are to

Commemorate, for the generations

to come you shall *Celebrate* it

as a *Festival* to the Lord—

a lasting *Ordinance.*

—Exodus 12:14—

Inspirations

Your thoughts, ideas, notes, hopes, goals, plans, potentials, etc....

Monthly Goals

SPIRITUAL

FAMILY

CAREER

HEALTH

Steps to Achieve My Goals

October

SUNDAY	MONDAY	TUESDAY	WEDNESDAY

Year: _____

THURSDAY	FRIDAY	SATURDAY	TO DO LIST
			•
			•
			•
			•
			•
			•
			•
			•
			•
			NOTES

My Budget

Monthly Income

Monthly Savings

Item Source	Amount	Date	Amount

Monthly Expenses

Item	Due Date	Amount
Rent/Mortgage		
Electric		
Gas		
Cell Phone		
Groceries		
Car Payment		
Auto Expenses		
Personal Care		
Entertainment		
Student Loans		
Credit Cards		
Miscellaneous		

Summary

Total Monthly Income	Total Monthly Expenses	Total Monthly Savings	Cash Balance

Shopping List

Grocery List	All other shopping needs

Notes:

This Month I Was Challenged to:

_____
_____
_____
_____
_____
_____
_____
_____
_____
_____
_____
_____
_____
_____
_____
_____
_____
_____

I Can do all this through *Him* who gives me *Strength.*

-Philippians 4:13-

Monthly Affirmation From God's Word:

What does God say is true about you?

I am... - I will... - God is...

_____

_____

_____

_____

_____

_____

_____

_____

_____

_____

_____

_____

_____

_____

_____

_____

_____

_____

I say to myself, "The _LORD_ is my _Portion_; therefore I will wait for him.

-Lamentations 3:24-

November

Praise the Lord.

Give Thanks to the Lord,

for he is Good;

his Love endures Forever.

—Psalm 106:1—

Inspirations

Your thoughts, ideas, notes, hopes, goals, plans, potentials, etc....

Monthly Goals

SPIRITUAL

FAMILY

CAREER

HEALTH

Steps to Achieve My Goals

November

SUNDAY	MONDAY	TUESDAY	WEDNESDAY

Year: _____

THURSDAY	FRIDAY	SATURDAY	TO DO LIST
			•
			•
			•
			•
			•
			•
			•
			•
			•
			NOTES

My Budget

Monthly Income   Monthly Savings

Item Source	Amount	Date	Amount

Monthly Expenses

Item	Due Date	Amount
Rent/Mortgage		
Electric		
Gas		
Cell Phone		
Groceries		
Car Payment		
Auto Expenses		
Personal Care		
Entertainment		
Student Loans		
Credit Cards		
Miscellaneous		

Summary

Total Monthly Income	Total Monthly Expenses	Total Monthly Savings	Cash Balance

Shopping List

Grocery List   All other shopping needs

Notes:

This Month I Was Challenged to:

_____

_____

_____

_____

_____

_____

_____

_____

_____

_____

_____

_____

_____

_____

_____

_____

_____

I Can do all this through *Him* who gives me *Strength.*

-Philippians 4:13-

Monthly Affirmation From God's Word:

What does God say is true about you?

I am... - I will... - God is...

_____

_____

_____

_____

_____

_____

_____

_____

_____

_____

_____

_____

_____

_____

_____

_____

_____

I say to myself, "The _LORD_ is my _Portion_; therefore I will wait for him.

-Lamentations 3:24-

December

For to us a *Child is Born*, to us a *Son* is given,

and the *Government* will be

on his *Shoulders*. And he will be called

Wonderful Counselor, *Mighty God*,

Everlasting *Father*, Prince of *Peace*.

—Isaiah 9:6—

Inspirations

Your thoughts, ideas, notes, hopes, goals, plans, potentials, etc....

Monthly Goals

SPIRITUAL

FAMILY

CAREER

HEALTH

Steps to Achieve My Goals

December

SUNDAY	MONDAY	TUESDAY	WEDNESDAY

Year: _____

THURSDAY	FRIDAY	SATURDAY	TO DO LIST

TO DO LIST

-
-
-
-
-
-
-
-
-

NOTES

My Budget

Monthly Income   Monthly Savings

Item Source	Amount	Date	Amount

Monthly Expenses

Item	Due Date	Amount
Rent/Mortgage		
Electric		
Gas		
Cell Phone		
Groceries		
Car Payment		
Auto Expenses		
Personal Care		
Entertainment		
Student Loans		
Credit Cards		
Miscellaneous		

Summary

Total Monthly Income	Total Monthly Expenses	Total Monthly Savings	Cash Balance

Shopping List

Notes:

This Month I Was Challenged to:

_____

_____

_____

_____

_____

_____

_____

_____

_____

_____

_____

_____

_____

_____

_____

_____

I Can do all this through *Him* who gives me *Strength.*

-Philippians 4:13-

Monthly Affirmation From God's Word:

What does God say is true about you?

I am... - I will... - God is...

_____

_____

_____

_____

_____

_____

_____

_____

_____

_____

_____

_____

_____

_____

_____

_____

_____

_____

_____

_____

_____

_____

I say to myself, "The LORD is my Portion; therefore I will wait for him.

-Lamentations 3:24-

CPSIA information can be obtained
at www.ICGtesting.com
Printed in the USA
LVHW071942161022
730832LV00031B/1723